United Nations –
Peacekeeper?

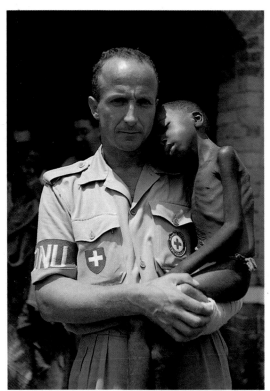

Edward Johnson

Thomson Learning • New York

Global Issues series

Genetic Engineering

Terrorism

UN—Peacekeeper?

The publishers would like to thank Sue Scarfe for her help in preparing this book for publication.

First published in the United States in 1995 by
Thomson Learning
New York, NY

Published simultaneously in Great Britain by
Wayland (Publishers) Ltd.

Library of Congress Cataloging-in-Publication Data
Johnson, Edward James, 1950–
United Nations—peacekeeper? / Edward Johnson.
    p.   cm.—(Global issues series)
  Includes bibliographical references and index.
  ISBN 1-56847-267-6
  1. United Nations—Armed Forces—Juvenile literature.
  [1. United Nations—Armed Forces.] I. Title. II. Series.
JX1981.P7J63   1995
341.5'84—dc20   95-6340

Printed in Italy

Picture Acknowledgments

Camera Press *title page* (T. Spencer), 8, 10, 11, 12 (L. Skoogfors), 14, 15, 20 (J. Haillot/*L'Express*), 21 (*Israel Sun*), 41, 48 (Benoit Gysembergh), 49 (Fiona McDougall), 53 (Benoit Gysembergh), 54 (Gavin Smith), 55 (Benoit Gysembergh); Topham 9 (R. Frehm), 13, 17, 24, 25, 29, 30, 31, 33, 36 (S. Lyon/STF), 37 (P. Northall), 40, 44 (E. F. Marti), 45 (S. Ratkovic), 52 (H. Krauss); United Nations *cover* (141245/J. Isaac), 6, 7, 16, 18, 19, 22 (Y. Nagata), 23 (M. Tzovaras), 26 (161894/Saw Lwin), 27 (156744/M. Grant), 29 (157214/M. Grant), 32 (157089), 34 (159185/P. Sudhakaran), 35 (159456/P. Sudhakaran), 38 (159301/J. Isaac), 39 (159283/J. Isaac), 42 (159301/J. Isaac), 43 (182009/M. Tzovaras), 50 (182120), 51 (159384/M. Grant), 56 (135526), 57 (186266), 58 (87491), 59 (174139).

Cover: A Norwegian soldier from the United Nations Interim Force in Lebanon (UNIFIL) on duty at an observation post in southern Lebanon. UNIFIL was created in 1978 to help restore peace and security in Lebanon and to make sure that Israeli troops had withdrawn from the area.

Title page: A neutral UN member in the Congo (now Zaire) in 1960 helps a small victim of the civil war.

CONTENTS

United Nations peacekeeping

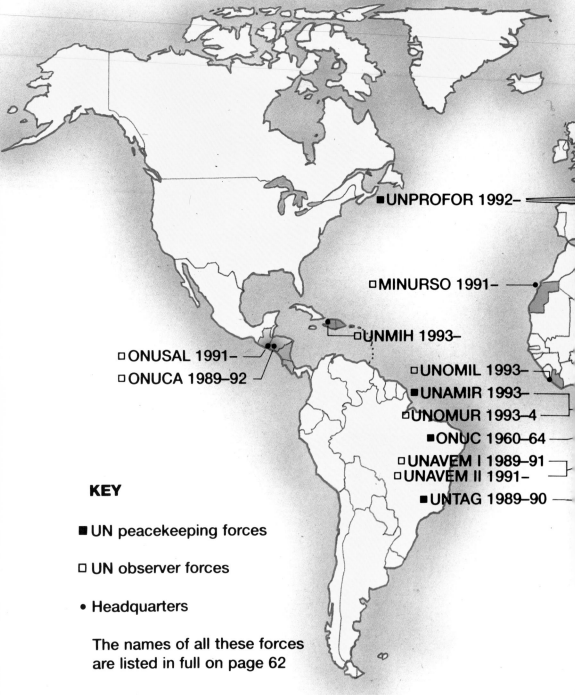

■UNPROFOR 1992–

□MINURSO 1991–

□UNMIH 1993–

□ONUSAL 1991–
□ONUCA 1989–92

□UNOMIL 1993–
■UNAMIR 1993–
□UNOMUR 1993–4
■ONUC 1960–64
□UNAVEM I 1989–91
□UNAVEM II 1991–
■UNTAG 1989–90

KEY

■ UN peacekeeping forces

□ UN observer forces

• Headquarters

The names of all these forces are listed in full on page 62

and observer forces since 1945

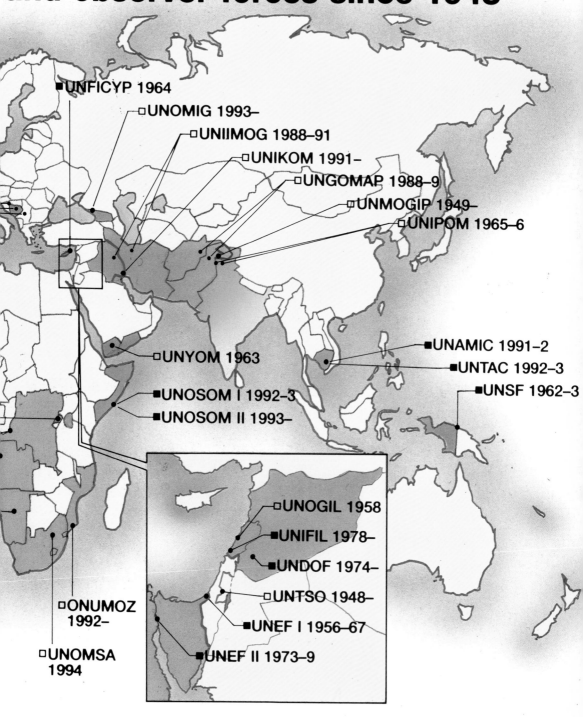

UNFICYP 1964

UNOMIG 1993–

UNIIMOG 1988–91

UNIKOM 1991–

UNGOMAP 1988–9

UNMOGIP 1949–

UNIPOM 1965–6

UNAMIC 1991–2

UNTAC 1992–3

UNSF 1962–3

UNYOM 1963

UNOSOM I 1992–3

UNOSOM II 1993–

ONUMOZ 1992–

UNOMSA 1994

UNOGIL 1958

UNIFIL 1978–

UNDOF 1974–

UNTSO 1948–

UNEF I 1956–67

UNEF II 1973–9

INTRODUCTION

In 1945, at the end of World War II, the victorious powers of the United States, Great Britain, and the Soviet Union came together to take the lead in forming the United Nations (UN). This body now includes among its members almost all the nations throughout the world. Its main purpose is the maintenance of world peace and the avoidance of war.

Since 1945, however, there have been numerous wars across the globe that have resulted in millions of casualties. It might seem that the UN has not been very successful in bringing peace to the world.

In 1949, members of the UN General Assembly are addressed by President Harry S. Truman during the ceremony of the laying of the cornerstone of the UN's permanent headquarters in New York City.

Harry S. Truman addresses the delegates from 50 nations attending the San Francisco Conference in 1945. The UN was organized during this conference.

Yet the UN can only do what its members—the major powers in particular—allow it to do. The fact that nations continue to war is not the fault of the UN. Some states continue to look for solutions to their problems through war and violence rather than through peaceful means. Despite its shortcomings, the UN has provided some useful services to a number of communities through the work of its peacekeeping forces. UN soldiers and police, in their distinctive blue berets and white vehicles, have, since the late 1980s, become familiar sights in trouble spots throughout the world.

UN peacekeepers have patrolled borders between hostile states; monitored elections and assisted states to reach independence; distributed humanitarian aid; and tried to calm—and even control—civil wars. These are only some of the wide range of roles performed by UN peacekeepers, but these are the roles we shall explore in this book.

> **66 99**
> • • •
>
> In 1946 British Prime Minister Clement Attlee said that the aim of those setting up the United Nations was "...not just the negation [abolition] of war, but the creation of a world of security and freedom, of a world which is governed by justice and the moral law. We desire to assert the pre-eminence of right over might and the general good against selfish and sectional aims."

ENFORCING PEACE

In 1945 the founders of the UN expected that the organization would maintain international peace by the very fact that countries would be working together, as allies, within it. If fighting did break out, the intention was that the major powers (the Soviet Union, the United States, Great Britain, France, and Nationalist China), which were all permanent members of the UN Security Council, would act together to stop the conflict. If necessary, the UN would intervene with armed forces to restore international peace and security. It was anticipated, therefore, that the UN would have forces of its own that it could send to a trouble spot to stop the fighting by military action. The UN would enforce peace whenever necessary.

The UN Security Council (right) debates the crisis that arose in the Persian Gulf after Iraq invaded Kuwait in 1991.

Missiles on show at a Soviet military parade (below). The staging of parades such as these showed the extent of the distrust and hostility among the major powers during the Cold War. This tense atmosphere hindered the workings of the UN.

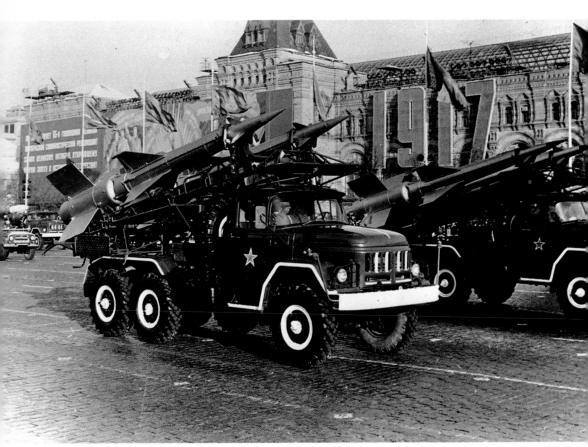

Fact File

The Security Council and the power of veto
The most important body in the UN is the Security Council. At present, it has fifteen members, five of which are permanent. These five permanent members are called the P5 and consist of the U.S., Russia (formerly the Soviet Union), Great Britain, France, and China. The other members of the Security Council serve for two years and are elected by the General Assembly, which is made up of representatives from all member states of the UN. One important difference between the permanent and the non-permanent members is that each of the permanent members has a veto. This means that if any one of them votes against a resolution made in the Security Council, that resolution cannot be adopted.

However, the UN quickly ran into difficulties. Relations among the major powers, particularly the United States and Great Britain on the one side and the Soviet Union on the other, worsened once World War II was over. There were many disagreements, and these countries, which had once been allies, sank into a deeply hostile relationship that, while it did not lead to open warfare, was sufficiently frosty to be termed the Cold War.

The UN was badly affected by the worsening relations among the major powers as the Cold War developed, and it was not given the authority or the armed forces that it was supposed to have to enforce international peace. Instead, the two opposing blocs in the Cold War developed their own means of maintaining security in the areas under their influence through the North Atlantic Treaty Organization (NATO) and the Warsaw Pact. The UN was left on the sidelines, and its authority became weakened. It could do little to establish peace in the face of divisions between the United States and the Soviet Union. This was particularly the case when the two superpowers supported different sides in any conflict, such as those in parts of Africa and Asia. The UN was kept from intervening in events by the superpowers, which sought peace on their own terms.

There have been, however, two instances of peace enforcement where the UN has supported direct military action, but these have been the exception rather than the rule. In both cases, the superpower opposition to enforcement was removed: in the first case by chance, and in the second as a result of the end of the Cold War and the improved relations between the superpowers after 1989. The first case was during the Korean War, fought from 1950 to 1953. The second was in the Gulf War, through Operation Desert Storm, in 1991.

U.S. troops, as part of the UN army, capture a North Korean position.

A U.S. soldier (right) interrogates a North Korean nurse during the Korean War. U.S. forces played the major role in the military operations that were approved by the UN Security Council.

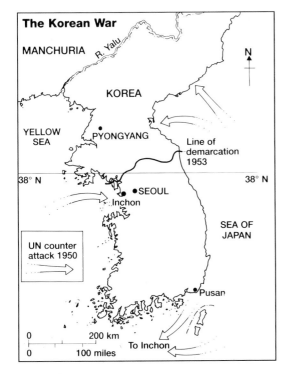

The Korean War

MANCHURIA

R. Yalu

KOREA

N

YELLOW
SEA

PYONGYANG

Line of
demarcation
1953

38° N

38° N

●SEOUL

Inchon

SEA OF
JAPAN

UN counter
attack 1950

Pusan

0   200 km

0   100 miles

To Inchon

Fact File

The Korean War
After the defeat of the Japanese forces in 1945, at the end of World War II, Korea was occupied jointly for a short time by the U.S. in the south and by the Soviet Union in the north. In 1947, a UN commission was sent to supervise free elections, but it was not allowed to enter the northern part of the country that was controlled by the Communists. In South Korea, the people elected a government headed by President Syngman Rhee; in North Korea, Kim Il Sung was proclaimed leader. Both governments claimed the right to control the whole country.

The North Korean army invaded South Korea in 1950, and the UN army found itself pushed all the way back to the southern tip of the country. Gradually, the UN troops managed to force the North Koreans up to the Chinese border. The military success of the UN army led China, which had turned Communist in 1949, to enter the war on the side of the North Koreans. Together, the North Koreans and the Chinese Communists forced the UN troops to retreat south. The fighting reached a stalemate at the 38th parallel (latitude 38° N). Both sides signed an armistice agreement and the forces remained facing each other, as they do to this day.

In June 1950, the army of the Communist government of North Korea crossed the border and invaded South Korea. The UN Security Council declared North Korea to be an aggressor and approved a force made up of troops from fifteen countries to intervene on behalf of the South Korean government. However, the UN was only able to authorize this force because the Soviet Union had temporarily withdrawn from the UN Security Council at the time, and therefore could not state its opposition to the UN action and use its power of veto. The action in Korea was peace enforcement, but it was carried out with a force that was not, strictly, a UN force, and the circumstances were unusual. It is helpful to think of the UN action in the Korean War as an operation led by the United States which used the UN as a means of gaining support for its actions. The UN operation in Korea was not paid for from UN funds, and the force received its orders from the U.S.-appointed military commander, not the UN Secretary General. There is no doubt that, had the Soviet Union been able to use its veto, the UN would not have approved this action.

Bomb damage in Iraq (right) caused by the coalition forces during Operation Desert Storm in 1991. Iraqi civilians inspect a huge bomb crater, which has filled with water.

The Gulf War

This example of peace enforcement in Korea in the early days of the Cold War was unusual, and the UN had to wait until the Cold War had ended before it was able to authorize such action again.

U.S. troops training in the desert before the beginning of Operation Desert Storm

In August 1990, the Iraqi army crossed over the border into Kuwait and illegally occupied the country. The United States felt this invasion threatened both the U.S. and the world economy, which depended on cheap and reliable supplies of oil. It organized a loose coalition of nearly 30 countries, through the UN, to oppose Iraq politically and militarily. Russia (which retained the seat on the Security Council formerly belonging to the Soviet Union) was broadly prepared to go along with this and allow the UN to give its stamp of approval to the U.S. action.

Fact File

The invasion of Kuwait
Iraq had a long-standing claim to Kuwait, which is rich in oil. The immediate dispute between the two countries arose because Kuwait was selling its oil too cheaply on the world market. This undercut Iraq's oil prices. It was important for Iraq to keep the price of oil high because it needed the money to rebuild the country after its 1980–88 war with Iran.

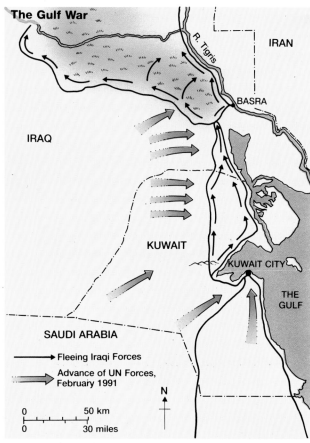

The Gulf War

IRAN

R. Tigris

BASRA

IRAQ

KUWAIT

KUWAIT CITY

THE GULF

SAUDI ARABIA

→ Fleeing Iraqi Forces

⇒ Advance of UN Forces, February 1991

N

0   50 km
0   30 miles

The U.S. was able to steer 12 resolutions against Iraq's occupation of Kuwait through the UN Security Council, and Russia supported all of them. The most significant of these was Resolution 678 of November 29, 1990. In this, the UN Security Council authorized the coalition of states to use force if Iraq did not withdraw its troops from Kuwait on or before January 15, 1991.

Operation Desert Storm

As a result of Resolution 678, the U.S. government was able to organize a large military force to carry out Operation Desert Storm. The Iraqi army was defeated and driven out of Kuwait. While most of the troops and equipment for this operation came from the United States, there were major contributions from France and Great Britain. In addition, before the land battle was actually fought, the allies launched a long bombing campaign against Iraq from military airfields in Turkey and in Arab states belonging to the coalition.

However, as with the peace enforcement action in Korea, the military operation was not paid for by the UN and the political decisions surrounding it were made not by the UN Secretary General but by the United States government. The main financial supporters of Operation Desert Storm were the Arab states opposed to Iraq, particularly Saudi Arabia, and other countries such as Japan and Germany.

Iraqi troops in Kuwait surrender to coalition forces on the second day of Operation Desert Storm, February 24,1991.

Military decisions were made by U.S. military commanders appointed by the United States President, not by the UN Secretary General. The Security Council had no control over the operation once Resolution 678 had been passed by the UN.

In Korea and the Gulf War, peace enforcement through the UN was possible because, for different reasons, the United States and the Soviet Union, and later Russia, did not block each other in the UN. In the case of Korea, it was purely by accident that the Soviet Union was not in a position to oppose the United States. In the case of the Gulf War, the ending of the Cold War in 1989 had produced better relations between the United States and Russia and a desire to cooperate more closely in the UN.

Kuwaiti women celebrating the victory of the coalition forces against Iraq and the liberation of their country. They are carrying Kuwaiti flags and pictures of the ruler of Kuwait, who was then still in exile.

PEACEKEEPING— CALMING COMBATANTS

Because the Cold War prevented the UN from enforcing peace in the way it had originally planned, the UN looked for other ways in which it might be able to intervene in conflicts. The UN organized two small, unarmed observer forces to help create stability: one in the Middle East in 1948, and another in Kashmir in 1949. These small forces were to be role models for future UN peacekeeping operations to follow.

The Suez crisis
The second UN Secretary General, Dag Hammarskjold (1953–61), saw an opportunity for UN action during the Suez Crisis of 1956. In that year, British, French, and Israeli armed forces had invaded Egypt, but they had been forced to end the fighting and to withdraw because of world opinion and diplomatic and economic pressure from the United States.

The United Nations Emergency Force (UNEF)
Against this background, the UN General Assembly asked Hammarskjold to organize UNEF, a small UN force made up of soldiers from ten countries. This force was sent to Egypt to supervise the withdrawal of the invading armies from Egyptian territory. It then moved on to the Egyptian-Israeli border where it observed a cease-fire between the two states, guarded essential installations, and reported on border incidents.

UN military observers in Kashmir as part of the United Nations Military Observer Group in India and Pakistan (UNMOGIP). At this time, the distinctive blue beret was not part of the UN uniform.

Fact File

Suez

In 1956, the Egyptian government, under President Nasser, nationalized the Suez Canal Company, which controlled the operation of the canal through Egyptian territory. The British and French governments, which each owned part of the Canal, were opposed to this action. They wished to see Nasser removed and the canal placed, once again, under international ownership. However, the United States did not wish to see force used in the Middle East, nor to see Nasser overthrown.

As a way around the U.S. position, the British and French joined with the Israeli government in a top secret plan. Israel invaded Egypt and advanced toward the canal. At this point, the British and French issued an ultimatum to both Israel and Egypt to stop fighting. The Israelis, as planned, called a halt, but Egypt did not. This gave the British and French an excuse to invade Egypt.

There seems no doubt that, during its 11-year stay—from 1956 to 1967—UNEF helped to keep peace in the Middle East. Its presence on the Egyptian-Israeli border discouraged either side from firing, and thus helped to reduce tension.

French invasion forces patrol Port Said in Egypt during the Suez War before the deployment of UNEF.

Until 1967, both Egypt and Israel saw the advantage of having UNEF on the border (although UNEF was only able to patrol the Egyptian side of the border, because the Israelis refused to have UN forces in their territory). In addition, UNEF had the advantage of operating in conditions that were helpful to peacekeeping operations. In the Sinai Desert, unhampered by trees, mountains, built-up areas, or bad weather conditions, it was easy to observe military movements by either side.

The Egyptians welcome the UNEF forces as they arrive in the Gaza Strip in 1957.

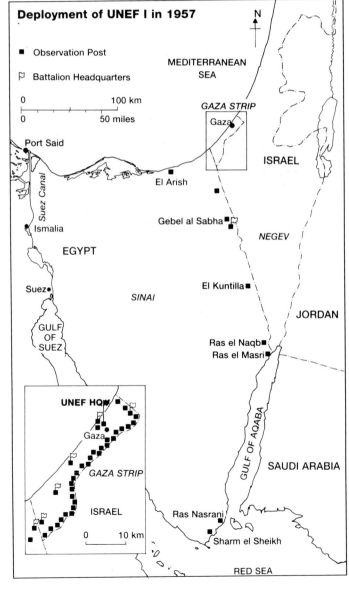

Deployment of UNEF I in 1957

The nature of UN peacekeeping

The UN force performed these duties successfully until 1967 when, at the request of the Egyptian government, it was withdrawn. The third Arab-Israeli war, often called the Six-Day War (because that is how long it took for the Israelis to defeat the Arabs) followed. The UN was criticized at the time for removing the UN peacekeeping force, but one of the main characteristics of UN peacekeeping is that the UN can operate only with the agreement of the warring states or parties in a dispute. This distinguishes UN *peacekeeping* from *peace enforcement*. The idea of UN peacekeeping is built on the belief that the UN should assist in the creation of peace, and it cannot do so without the agreement and support of the conflicting parties. When the Egyptian government withdrew its consent in 1967, the UN was obliged to withdraw its force.

Members of the Yugoslavian contingent of UNEF observing the Egyptian-Israeli cease-fire line in the Sinai peninsula near the Gulf of 'Aqaba.

The need for the consent of the warring parties before UN peacekeepers can act is not the only feature of UN peacekeeping. UN peacekeepers must keep a neutral position; it can't take sides with any of the warring parties. Finally, UN peacekeeping forces are generally small compared with the armies involved in the actual conflict, and their policy is to appear as nonthreatening as possible.

Troop movements in Sinai during the Six-Day War

The first UN force in Egypt was never more than six thousand troops. Only the large UN peacekeeping forces—those in the Congo (now Zaire) from 1960 to 1964, those in the former Yugoslavia from 1992 to 1994, and the UN force in Somalia during 1993 and 1994—have exceeded 20,000. In addition, UN peacekeeping forces are only lightly armed and the small observer forces are unarmed, so they do not pose a significant military threat to the parties in a conflict.

The Yom Kippur War
It was the removal of UNEF in 1967 that led to the Six-Day War. After this conflict came to an end, there was an uneasy peace between Israel and its Arab neighbors for a number of years. In 1973, however, the Egyptians and the Syrians attacked the Israelis without warning on a Jewish holy day, the Day of Atonement, Yom Kippur.

Israeli tanks on the move during the Yom Kippur War

Fact File

The Yom Kippur War

The 1967 Six-Day War was a disaster for the Arabs. Israel gained much Arab territory, including the Sinai Peninsula and the west bank of the Jordan River.

So, after a number of years rebuilding their arms supplies and with a new leader in the Arab world, President Anwar Sadat of Egypt, the Arabs launched an attack on the Israelis on Yom Kippur, October 1973. For a time, it looked as though the Arabs would win, since the Israelis had to fight a war on two fronts: against the Egyptians and against the Syrians. After two weeks of fighting, however, the Israelis had not only driven the Syrians back, but had also crossed deep into Egyptian territory and cut off part of the Egyptian army from retreat. In this situation, the United States and the Soviet Union set up negotiations to end the hostilities. As part of the agreed cease-fire between Israel and the Arabs, two UN peacekeeping forces were established: UNEF II and UNDOF. UNEF II was withdrawn in 1979 after a peace treaty was signed between Egypt and Israel. UNDOF is still in position.

The United Nations Disengagement Observer Force (UNDOF)

The UN was asked to establish peacekeeping forces to separate the Israelis from both the Egyptians and the Syrians. In 1974, UNEF II was set up to operate along the Israeli-Egyptian border, and UNDOF began operating on the Israeli-Syrian border. Although it is called an observer force, it is, in fact, a large, lightly-armed peacekeeping force. It has successfully performed a number of tasks since it was established.

A Finnish member of UNEF II on observation duty in 1974. This observation post is in the buffer zone between Egyptian and Israeli troops, which was established after the Yom Kippur War.

UNDOF's first task was to ensure that Israel withdrew from most of the Syrian territory that it had captured in the 1973 war. The Israelis pulled their troops back as agreed, and the UN force was put in between the Israelis and the Syrians as a barrier for peace. The Israelis continued to hold the hills, formerly in Syria, called the Golan Heights. These are very important strategically because they overlook the fertile and prosperous northern part of the small state of Israel.

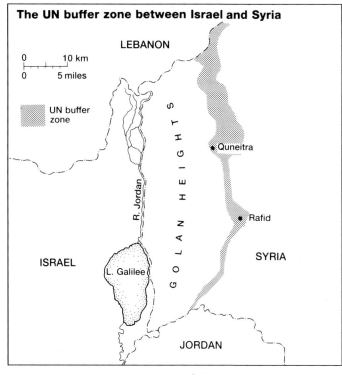

The UN buffer zone between Israel and Syria

LEBANON

0   10 km
0   5 miles

UN buffer zone

GOLAN HEIGHTS

Quneitra

R. Jordan

Rafid

ISRAEL

L. Galilee

SYRIA

JORDAN

The UN Security Council renewing the mandate of UNDOF for six months in November 1975. On this occasion, as the picture shows, the Chinese and Iraqi delegates refused to vote on the resolution.

The Syrian army is now physically separated from the Golan Heights by a buffer zone in which the UN force operates. Both sides have a limited number of weapons and soldiers that are allowed to be positioned within a distance of about 14 miles from either side of this zone.

The UN force also checks on the level of weapons held by Israel and Syria on either side of this zone. In this way, the UN force has been able to reduce the tension between the two states.

A member of UNDOF oversees the cease-fire on the Israel-Syria border in 1973 after the Yom Kippur War.

UNDOF has been helped in its tasks by the fact that both Syria and Israel accept the presence of the force operating within the buffer zone. The Israelis have supported UNDOF because its activities have helped to stabilize the border, and in doing so has allowed the Israelis to continue to occupy the Golan Heights, which they consider vital to their security. In this way, the UN presence has frozen the dispute to the advantage of one side. However, the Syrians have shown no desire to overrun the UN positions and disrupt the calm, as they have no wish to start another war with Israel. Moreover, they have a long-running political dispute with Iraq on their eastern border that occupies much of their attention. In this case, therefore, the UN's role has been broadly supported by both sides. UNDOF has been helped by the absence of any other regular or irregular armed groups that could have caused difficulties for the UN in this area of the Middle East. Neither the Israelis nor the Syrians have always allowed UNDOF complete freedom of movement when it is trying to observe the level of weapons in the area on either side of the buffer zone, but this has not caused too many problems. Like UNEF and UNEF II, UNDOF has been helped by the fact that the landscape and the weather conditions are ideal for the successful performance of its tasks.

Difficulties faced by the UN in its peacekeeping role
UNEF, UNEF II, and UNDOF were able to operate because, after 1945 the Middle East became the center of major conflicts in international politics. The superpowers were prepared to allow the UN a role so that the troubles in the Middle East would not spread and threaten their own security. Yet, throughout the Cold War, the superpowers did not allow UN peacekeeping to operate in other areas if it clashed with their interests. The United States did not, for example, allow the UN to intervene in the war in Vietnam, which lasted from 1960 to 1975. In the invasion of Hungary in 1956 and Czechoslovakia in 1968, the Soviet Union kept the UN from playing any role.

Hungarian citizens fighting against their Soviet-style Communist government in 1956. The Soviet Union sent in troops and tanks to crush the uprising and refused to allow the UN to intervene.

Other factors also kept the UN from developing its peacekeeping role at this time. The UN needed adequate funds to finance its peacekeeping tasks and a supply of soldiers willing to serve in its forces. Neither of these were immediately available, and, as this book will show, these factors have been crucial to the development of the UN peacekeeping role since its inception.

PEACEKEEPING— ASSISTING TRANSITION

The division between the superpowers was one of the main factors that restricted the UN's peacekeeping opportunities during the Cold War. When relations improved between the United States and the Soviet Union in the late 1980s, the two countries at last began to cooperate to a much greater extent in the UN. Previously, there had been an atmosphere of suspicion and hostility between them. After the Cold War, the UN could play a more active role in international politics, and it is now clear that UN peacekeepers are in demand around the world.

Javier Perez de Cuellar, the fifth UN Secretary General, arriving in Angola in August 1983 after visiting South Africa to discuss the UN plan for Namibia. Members of the crowd carry placards supporting the plan, which was executed in 1989.

In the 1980s the Soviet Union, under President Mikhail Gorbachev, began to pay its share for UN peacekeeping, which it had previously refused to do. The Soviet Union even allowed a small UN force to help the Soviet Army withdraw from Afghanistan from 1988 to 1990. The U.S. government also started to pay off its outstanding debts to the UN and there was, therefore, a more constructive and agreeable atmosphere in the UN Security Council. This was especially true among the five permanent members of the council—the United States, the Soviet Union (Russia after 1991), Great Britain, France, and the People's Republic of China. This cooperation led to the creation of more than 20 UN peacekeeping operations between 1987 and 1993. These new operations often gave the UN forces wider responsibilities than before. In addition, the UN has also felt able to expand the scope of peacekeeping. For example, some operations in the 1990s involved the UN's using force to try to achieve its agreed objectives, and not merely to defend itself. This chapter, together with the next two chapters, deals with examples of these developments.

Namibia

South Africa had illegally occupied Namibia since World War II, when it had refused to put the country under the trusteeship of the UN. A plan for independence had been drawn up in 1978, but no progress could be made until the Cold War had ended and both the Soviet Union and the United States could join together, with other countries, to put pressure on the South African government.

Perez de Cuellar inspecting the Kenyan contingent of UNTAG in Namibia in 1989. General Prem Chand, the force commander, accompanies him.

Fact File

Namibia

Before World War I, Namibia (then called South West Africa) was a German colony. After the war, it was governed by South Africa under the League of Nations. After the UN was founded, it wanted to give South West Africa its independence but the South African government refused to allow this. The UN renamed the area Namibia and, in the 1970s, approved a resolution calling for free elections and recognizing the South West Africa People's Organization (SWAPO) as the true representatives of the Namibian people. In 1978, a settlement plan was created that aimed for Namibian independence, but the South Africans would not leave the area. Part of the reason was that to the north of Namibia, in Angola, there was a civil war taking place in which Soviet-backed Cuban troops were fighting. The South Africans feared that Communism would spread into southern Africa, and they thought Namibia would act as a barrier against this. They also felt that if Namibia became independent, Communism might gain a foothold in that territory. By 1988, the situation in Angola had changed and the Cold War had ended. South Africa agreed to leave Namibia and the settlement plan was put into operation.

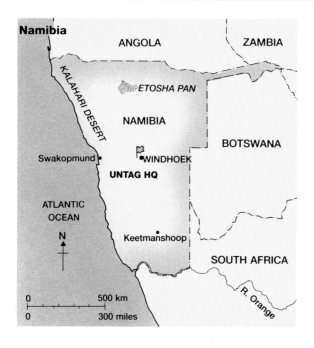

Namibia

66 99

• • •

"The UN attaches the highest importance to the Namibian question…and is determined that the people of the Territory be enabled to exercise their right to self-determination and independence in a free, fair, and democratic manner."

Source: UN Secretary General Perez de Cuellar on arriving in South Africa in August 1983 for talks with the government on Namibia

Finnish peacekeepers (above) arrive in Namibia aboard a U.S. Galaxy transport aircraft.

Members of UNTAG (left) carry a wounded SWAPO guerrilla to a helicopter in April 1989.

The United Nations Transition Assistance Group (UNTAG) 1989–90

UNTAG was created in 1989 to help Namibia become independent from South Africa and to help carry out the 1978 plan for independence. This force had to deal with a range of problems that could have prevented Namibia from moving peacefully to independence. It was made up of a number of military and civilian sections, each designed to deal with a particular difficulty.

The military sections included a peacekeeping force and an observer unit. The peacekeeping force was made up of three infantry battalions, while the observer unit was made up of three hundred military observers from a number of states. The civilian sections were made up of election observers and civilian police, who were there to help keep law and order.

The military sections had various duties to perform. The first was to make sure that the number of military units operating within Namibia was reduced. This involved checking that the South African Defense Force (SADF), which numbered 30,000 in 1989, was withdrawing as planned. It also involved ensuring that the guerrilla forces of SWAPO, which had fought the SADF for independence, were disarmed and would return to their bases in the adjoining countries of Angola and Zambia. The UN wanted the SADF to have no excuse to intervene again in Namibia.

Members of the British contingent to UNTAG on patrol in Namibia in 1989

The second task was to keep Namibia free from any outside interference while it moved toward independence. UNTAG military units were posted along Namibia's borders to make sure that groups of people that might want to cause trouble were not allowed to enter the country.

However, at the very beginning, UNTAG personnel were scarce. When SWAPO guerrillas crossed over the border from Angola into Namibia, threatening the free elections, UNTAG was not strong enough to hold them back. As a partial solution, the UN allowed the SADF to stop the SWAPO advance. However, this was a dangerous course of action, because UNTAG's neutral position could have been brought in to question. A new cease-fire was agreed only after much diplomatic activity, which went on for many weeks, and the SWAPO guerrillas were persuaded to return to their bases. This dangerous situation had happened because of attempts to save money on the use of UN forces, and SWAPO had intervened at a time when those forces were weak. UNTAG then had to make sure that the new cease-fire between the SWAPO and the SADF held so that conditions for the elections would be stable and peaceful.

SWAPO troops killed by the SADF in the border areas of Namibia in September 1989. The South Africans continued to operate in Namibia until October 1989.

Elections in Namibia were held under UN supervision. Here are some of the electoral monitors at work.

The civilian section of UNTAG was made up of a group of electoral monitors and a large civilian police force. The electoral monitors were there to establish procedures for the elections and to explain to the Namibians, who had never voted before, how the elections would be carried out. During the elections in November 1989, the monitors were present to make sure that they were held in a correct fashion—free, fair, and without corruption—and that the voters were not intimidated or threatened.

The civilian police were made part of UNTAG to help maintain law and order and to monitor the activities of the South West Africa Police (SWAPOL) which was controlled by South Africa. People were afraid that SWAPOL would try to undermine the elections, so by October 1989, UNTAG's police force was increased from 500 to 1,500. UNTAG police were often viewed with hostility by the local police, but they were able to ensure the registration of about 700,000 voters for the elections. Of these, almost 98 percent actually voted in the November 7–11, 1989 elections.

UNTAG's operations in Namibia were highly successful, and it was the first peacekeeping operation of its kind that was given the responsibility of assisting a state to become independent. The civilian sections of UNTAG were essential to the success of the UN operation, as was the political support it received from a number of states, all of which hoped UNTAG would succeed. Namibia gained independence March 21, 1990.

Cambodia

UNTAG's success in preparing Namibia for independence encouraged the UN to send a peacekeeping force to Cambodia.

SWAPO supporters await the election results in Namibia.

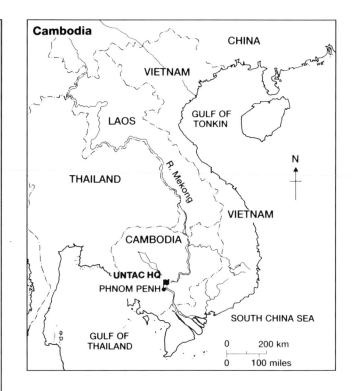

The United Nations Transitional Authority in Cambodia (UNTAC)

In 1989, the various groups that had been fighting for control in Cambodia agreed to allow the UN to observe elections to choose a new government. UNTAC, a mixed force of 22,000 military, police, and civilian personnel, was sent to Cambodia in March 1992. It had many different tasks and the operation was the most ambitious peacekeeping enterprise the UN had ever undertaken. UNTAC's duties included overseeing the cease-fire among

the four warring groups and disarming them, clearing mines, providing election monitors to oversee the April-May 1993 elections for a new Cambodian government, and supplying civilian workers to administer many areas of government in the time leading up to the elections. In this program, UN peacekeepers took on new roles. Before this, UN peacekeepers had not become involved in the government of the country to which they had been sent. For a brief while before the elections, the UN force governed Cambodia.

Cambodian refugees returning from Thailand in 1992 to vote under UN protection.

Members of the Khmer People's National Liberation Armed Forces (left) waiting to be disarmed by the UN force in Cambodia, 1992

By 1994, most of the UNTAC personnel had left the country and a new Cambodian government was in place. A guerrilla campaign was still being fought in parts of the country by the forces of the Khmer Rouge, but Cambodia was in a far more stable and peaceful condition than it had been before UNTAC arrived.

PEACEKEEPING—MODERATING CIVIL WARS

The UN in former Yugoslavia

The previous chapter showed an example of successful internal peacekeeping by UN forces while helping Namibia to gain independence. The focus of this chapter will again be on internal peacekeeping, where the UN has been involved in trying to calm a civil war in some areas of the former Yugoslavia.

Yugoslavia, with its unstable mixture of different nationalities, religions, languages, and traditions, became a Communist country under the strong leadership of Marshal Tito after World War II. Tito died in 1980. By 1989, Communism was in decline across the whole of Eastern Europe, including the Soviet Union. Once the old Communist Party had lost its power in Yugoslavia, cultural and religious differences and the old, bitter rivalries came to the surface. The country began to break up into smaller, separate states.

The victim of a sniper's bullet lies dead in Sarajevo, the capital of Bosnia, in 1992.

The provinces of Yugoslavia

KEY

- ◪ Serbs
- ◪ Croats
- ▤ Macedonians
- ▤ Montenegrins
- ▥ Slovenes
- ▨ Moslems

```
0        100 km
0        50 miles
```

HUNGARY

N

SLOVENIA
● Ljubljana
● Zagreb
CROATIA
VOJVODINA
● Novi Sad
● Belgrade
ROMANIA

○ ○ BOSNIA
HERCEGOVINA
Sarajevo ●
SERBIA

ADRIATIC
SEA

MONTENEGRO ● Pristina
Titograd ● KOSOVO
BULGARIA

ITALY
● Skopje
MACEDONIA
ALBANIA
GREECE

Fact File

Yugoslavia

Yugoslavia became an independent state at the end of World War I. It was formed from territories that were once part of the Empire of Austria–Hungary and from the kingdoms of Serbia and Bosnia–Herzegovina, two states that had belonged to the Turkish Empire from the 15th and 16th centuries.

From the start, Yugoslavia was not a unified state. It was made up of six regions: Serbia, Croatia, Slovenia, Bosnia, Macedonia, and Montenegro. Within these regions, there were distinct national areas such as Serbia, but Serbs also lived in parts of Croatia and Bosnia. Yugoslavia was also divided by religion: the Croats and Slovenes were mainly Roman Catholic, while the Serbs were Serbian Orthodox (a sect of the Eastern Orthodox church) and the Bosnians were Muslim.

A UN plane lands at Sarajevo airport as a UN convoy awaits the Bosnian Serbs' permission to allow aid to be delivered to the besieged town of Gorazde, 1994

The United Nations Protection Force (UNPROFOR)

UNPROFOR was sent to Croatia in 1992 after a war had broken out between Serbia and Croatia. It was designed to separate those Serbs who had always lived in some parts of Croatia from the indigenous Croats after the war had ended. Its role was to promote calm and increase confidence between the two warring states.

In 1993, another part of the force was sent to Macedonia, in the south, to discourage any ethnic conflict from spreading from Serbia into Macedonia. If this had happened, all the Balkan states could have been dragged into a war that would have involved Greece, Albania, and Bulgaria, as well as former Yugoslavia. This second part of the force was engaged in what UN Secretary General Boutros-Ghali called "preventive deployment": the aim of this was to discourage rival groups and armed bands from fighting.

A Croatian villager trying to contact relatives in the town of Split asks for help from the UN civilian police 1992.

A third part of the UN force, which operated in Bosnia, was the one that gained the most attention and experienced the most difficulties. In early 1992, after Bosnia declared itself independent, a civil war broke out involving Bosnian Serbs, Bosnian Croats, and Bosnian Muslims. The Serbs and Croats were hoping to expand the areas under their control by defeating the Bosnian Muslims and thus dividing most of Bosnia between themselves.

Many towns and cities, populated mainly by Muslims, were surrounded by armed Bosnian Serbs, determined to bring about the surrender of the Muslims and then move them by force to other parts of Bosnia. This practice became known as ethnic cleansing. Croat forces attacked other Muslim areas, and Muslim troops tried to capture areas populated by Croats. During this bitter civil war, everyday life in Bosnia broke down: towns were shelled, army snipers killed civilians in the streets, airports were shut down, and roads were closed. Large sections of the Bosnian population were held hostage in the towns, unable to escape or to live normal lives. It was very difficult for people to find food, and medical supplies began to run out.

A member of the Danish contingent to UNPROFOR on observation duties with the force in Croatia in 1992

Part of the British contingent of UNPROFOR leads a relief convoy with over 40 tons of food through Bosnia, November 1992.

Faced with this situation, the UN High Commission for Refugees and a number of international aid agencies organized relief supplies of food and essential materials to be sent to the besieged Bosnian people. It was often dangerous to deliver these goods to the trapped Bosnian Muslims. In order to reach their destinations, convoys of trucks had to be driven from the coast on bad, mountain roads that were patrolled by Serbian and Croatian troops. Often these patrols were hostile and obstructive. Without protection, the relief supplies could not get through to the starving and desperate people who needed them. Eventually, UNPROFOR was given the responsibility of protecting these supply convoys.

The role of UNPROFOR in Bosnia
The Bosnian Muslims hoped UNPROFOR would be able to lift the siege of many of the towns and prevent the destruction of their country. However, they were soon to be disappointed, and dissatisfaction with the UN force spread quickly. UNPROFOR could not use

force to protect them, because it was not permitted to do so by the UN Security Council or by the governments who had contributed troops to the operation.

UNPROFOR's role was limited to escorting the aid convoys. Since it was a peacekeeping force, it could use military force only in self-defense. The use of road blocks by Serbs and Croats to delay the delivery of aid caused a major problem and UNPROFOR had no solution to this. In the beginning, it had no authority to use force to push the shipments of aid through or to dismantle the road blocks. It could only negotiate with the Serbs and Croats, where possible, for the removal of obstructions to allow the aid through. If that was not possible, the essential food and medical supplies remained stranded on roads in Bosnia. This frustrating situation was made worse by the fact that the powerlessness of the UN was captured regularly on television cameras and transmitted across the world. It was not surprising, therefore, that UN Secretary General Boutros-Ghali was met by hostile Muslims when he visited Sarajevo in 1993.

Members of the French contingent of UNPROFOR inspect Lovinac, a village destroyed by Bosnian Serbs.

In an attempt to do something more positive for the Muslims, the UN Security Council passed a resolution in 1993 that permitted the UN to use force in order to get aid through. It also created a number of safe havens in besieged towns and surrounding areas in case they were attacked. In addition, the UN threatened the Serbs with air strikes if they continued to shell the towns. This resolution did not, however, assist the UN troops on the ground. Although they then had the legal right to use force, they did not have the necessary military resources to get involved in a shooting war with the Serb or Croat armies. The number of UNPROFOR troops in Bosnia in 1994 was only 22,000. The UN found it difficult to find more troops to serve in Bosnia, and those states that had provided troops were reluctant to approve air strikes or other military action because they feared reprisals against their own troops by the Serbs.

UN troops patrolling Sarajevo airport in 1992. The airport was later closed by Serbs who prevented supplies from reaching Sarajevo, an attempt to try to starve out the Bosnian Muslims.

The Security Council discusses imposing sanctions against Serbia and Montenegro in 1992 to try to stop them from supporting the Bosnian Serbs.

Media Watch

Terror in Gorazde

"My parents died when a shell blew through the wall of our apartment," said Elmira Zlatic, who escorted her 8-year-old brother to Sarajevo on a United Nations helicopter on Sunday.

"It was on a Tuesday," she said. "My father came back from the front, and my mother went up to make him something to eat."

On Saturday, Elmira ran with her brother to the hospital because the boy [was] traumatized by his parents' deaths. "It was at night, and we were not alone," she said. "We had to run for it because of the snipers and the shells, but it took a long time, even though it was only 100 meters."

Source: *New York Times*, April 26,1994

Media Watch

UN convoy blocked

The Serbs…warned that they would not allow a convoy of 141 United Nations troops and medical personnel to enter the Gorazde enclave until Bosnian Government forces withdrew at least two miles from the west bank of the Drina…This morning the Serbs had allowed the convoy, which included Ukrainian, British, and French troops and Norwegian medical workers, to leave Sarajevo for Gorazde. But 350 Serbian women and children near Rogatica blocked the convoy this afternoon. Serbian officials insisted that they were trying to convice the women to allow the convoy through. But women and children have frequently been recruited by Serbian fighters to block convoys headed to Muslim towns.

Source: *New York Times*, April 22,1994

UN soldiers inspect the site where a UN convoy was attacked by Bosnian Serbs near Sarajevo in July 1994.

The Bosnian Muslims felt that the UN was trying to keep them alive through aid deliveries only to allow them to be killed by Serb shells. Some Muslims believed that the UN was taking the side of the Serbs and Croats against them. However, the Serbs also accused the UN force of taking sides and charged the UN with delivering arms and weapons to the Muslims in the food convoys. The UN had imposed an arms embargo to try to stop weapon supplies to all the warring groups. The situation worked mostly against the Muslims, because the Serbs were able to use the military equipment of the former Yugoslav army, as well as arms they had received from parts of Eastern Europe. The Croats were able to get a supply of arms from parts of Western Europe. The arms embargo left only the Bosnian Muslims in a weak position.

By 1994 it was expected that the UN would have to withdraw its forces from Bosnia. There seemed to be no peace settlement acceptable to all parties, and morale in the force was low. While the UN had the authority to use force, there was no political will among member states to turn it into action. This led to disagreements between the UN Secretary General and the military commanders on the ground, some of whom wanted to use force against the Serbs. But political will changed in February 1994, when the Serbs shelled a food line in Sarajevo and killed over 70 civilians. The Serbs were told to remove their heavy guns and tanks from the area around Sarajevo or risk air strikes by NATO planes against them. These strikes would be carried out in

UN troops move a Bosnian Serb gun, 1994. This followed a UN/NATO ultimatum requiring that the Serbs remove heavy weapons from around Sarajevo.

support of the 1993 UN resolution. This first ultimatum had the desired effect, but it and others that followed, did little to force agreement to a peace settlement. In 1994, an international plan was drawn up to end the war, but the Bosnian Serbs refused to accept it. In November 1994, NATO air forces, in support of the UN, bombed Serb positions around the safe haven of Bihac in Bosnia after it had come under attack by Bosnian Serb forces. Former president Jimmy Carter then negotiated a cease-fire among the parties in Bosnia, but many people doubted that this would hold any better than the many previous ones had.

There were two broad views in response to all these difficulties. The first was that the UN should leave Bosnia because its presence was only delaying the inevitable. Serbs, Croats, and Bosnians would have to reach a settlement by themselves, and the intervention of the UN force was actually preventing this from happening. The other view was that, if the UN did withdraw, the war could spread to other parts of former Yugoslavia, such as Macedonia, and there could be the risk of a widespread Balkan war.

The experience of UNPROFOR shows the frustrations and difficulties that arise when a peacekeeping force is put into a situation such as a complex civil war without the necessary political and military support. If the UN were to try to enforce peace in Bosnia and go beyond the peacekeeping role, it would require a

Bosnia in November 1994

N

SLOVENIA

HUNGARY

● Zagreb

More than 1,000 Bangladeshi
UN peacekeepers in
Bihac enclave

CROATIA

VOJVODINA

● Erdut

Bosnian Serb attacks

● Orasje

● Bihac

Banja Luka ●

BOSNIA HERCEGOVINA

Tuzla ●

Belgrade
●

Ubdina ●

54 Canadian UN
peacekeepers detained
at Visoko by
Bosnian Serbs

● Zadar

Travnik ●
● Vitez

Visoko

SERBIA

● Srebrenica

G Vakuf ● ●

● Split

SARAJEVO

250 French, Ukrainian
and Canadian
peacekeepers
held hostage
around Sarajevo

● Gorazde

Mostar ●

MONTENEGRO

Muslims in Bosnia and Croatia

Serbs in Bosnia and Croatia

0   100 km

0   50 miles

ADRIATIC SEA

ALBANIA

commitment by states to provide an army of over
100,000 troops, possibly for a long period of time, and
certainly for years rather than months. In 1994 there
was not much evidence that member states of the UN
were prepared to make this commitment, because of
the political, financial, and military costs involved.
Some member states, particularly Russia, were uneasy
about the UN's authorizing air strikes against the Serbs.
In the next chapter we shall see what can happen when
the UN does use force.

Media Watch

Serbs set to sweep into Bihac

Fierce fighting raged today around the Muslim enclave ["safe area"] of Bihac in northwestern Bosnia when Serbian forces pursued a steady advance toward the center of the town and NATO allies failed to agree on how to save it.

In a move to discourage retaliatory bombings by NATO, Serbs immobilized about 200 United Nations troops and observers around Sarajevo and detained about 50 Canadian troops north of the capital. The tactic, used by the Serbs in the past when they faced air strikes, left the peacekeepers virtual hostages…

General conditions for the 180,000 people in the Bihac area remain dire.

Source: *New York Times*, November 25, 1994

Media Watch

The UN as scapegoat

United Nations, November 28—Secretary General Boutros Boutros-Ghali will fly to Sarajevo on Wednesday to try to meet with the leaders of the Bosnian Government and the rebel Bosnian Serbs in an effort to talk them into stopping their war, United Nations officials said tonight.

The officials said Mr. Boutros-Ghali would seek to meet either separately or together with President Alija Izetbegovic of Bosnia and Radovan Karadzic, the leader of the Bosnian Serbs.

The Secretary General sent letters early this afternoon to the two leaders proposing the meeting, but had not yet received a reply, said Joe Sills, Mr. Boutros-Ghali's spokesman.

The Secretary General's peace initiative came after the head of United Nations peacekeeping operations asserted that the United Nations was "being made a scapegoat" for not acting more forcefully in Bosnia. The official, Kofi Annan, insisted that ordering further military action was up to the member states but that he believed that they lacked a collective will to do so.

"I believe the UN is being made a scapegoat—of course we do have a scapegoat function," Mr. Annan said. "But it is absolutely unfair when member states do not want to take the risks—when they do not want to commit the resources—but blame the UN for failure to act."

Source: *New York Times,* November 29, 1994

PEACEKEEPING— CONTROLLING CIVIL WARS

Somalia

Somalia, in the Horn of Africa, became a focus of international concern after 1991 when the government of General Muhammad Siyad Barre was overthrown. This left the country extremely unstable. Widespread fighting broke out among different groups, headed by warlords, each struggling to take control of the state. This turned into civil war, and the country gradually descended into chaos. This disorder was accompanied by large-scale famine across the country. By the beginning of 1992, the situation in Somalia was desperate. Relief supplies in the form of food and medical necessities, organized by international charities, were only able to get through to their destinations with the agreement and cooperation of the local warlords who controlled different parts of the country. Many people fled across the borders as refugees.

A starving family in Somalia has managed to reach a food distribution center, 1992. Many people died of hunger because widespread disorder throughout the country disrupted the distribution of food supplies.

Fact File

Somalia

Somalia is strategically important because it overlooks the sea routes between the Red Sea and the Indian Ocean. During the Cold War, both the United States and the Soviet Union made use of the naval bases in Somalia and sold weapons to the Somali government. As a result, Somalia had a lot of weapons, and these got into the hands of tribal gangs. In 1991, Somali dictator Siyad Barre was overthrown by a rival, and civil war broke out between the different tribes under local warlords.

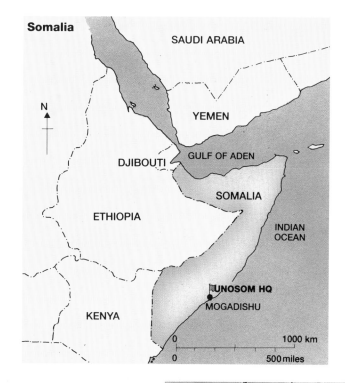

Somalia

SAUDI ARABIA

YEMEN

DJIBOUTI

GULF OF ADEN

SOMALIA

ETHIOPIA

INDIAN OCEAN

KENYA

UNOSOM HQ

MOGADISHU

0   1000 km

0   500 miles

Organized gangs loot relief supplies at one of Somalia's ports, 1992

The UN decided to assist in the distribution of the relief supplies. Acting under Chapter VII of the UN Charter, the Security Council passed a resolution in January 1992 imposing an arms embargo on Somalia. This was intended to keep the different factions in the civil war from obtaining further military supplies. In March of the same year, a cease-fire was arranged by the UN in Mogadishu, the capital of Somalia. The Secretary General then proposed that a small observer force be created to monitor the cease-fire. He also proposed that a 500-strong peacekeeping force be assembled to escort the relief supplies from Somalia's ports to distribution centers throughout the country.

United Nations Operation in Somalia (UNOSOM I)

The peacekeeping force UNOSOM I was organized on traditional lines. It therefore had, in theory, to act with the agreement of the government of the country in which it would operate. In Somalia, however, there was no host government, but a number of groups all claiming to have authority. In this situation, the UN had to convince the main warring groups to agree to the formation of the force. This took time; therefore, the main part of UNOSOM I did not begin to operate until September and October 1992. Following the arrival of the first troops, a Pakistani unit, in UNOSOM I, another resolution was passed that was intended to expand the numbers in the force. It was hoped that this would allow the force to extend its peacekeeping and escort functions over the whole of Somalia.

In December 1992, the Security Council voted unanimously to set up the Unified Task Force (UNITAF) under U.S. command. Its purpose was to make it possible to distribute food supplies more efficiently in Somalia.

Unfortunately, the UN force was never able to fulfill its tasks. The Pakistani troops in UNOSOM I were attacked by the warring factions and found it impossible either to protect the delivery of the relief supplies or to secure the cease-fire. Since other

Installing radio equipment into a jeep belonging to the Pakistani contingent to UNOSOM I, 1992. Communications were to be a major problem for the UN forces in Somalia.

countries were not willing to commit troops to Somalia, the force was never expanded. The civil war dragged on and many Somalis continued to die of starvation.

Operation Restore Hope
The U.S. government, therefore, proposed the creation of a task force under the command of the United States, not the UN, to go into Somalia. Its purpose would be to make sure that food and medical supplies were distributed, using force if necessary. In December 1992 the UN Security Council agreed to have this force set up, and the first U.S. troops were sent into Somalia under Operation Restore Hope.

As many as 29 countries joined the coalition under US command in the Unified Task Force (UNITAF). There were then two forces operating in Somalia: the small UNOSOM I, which was governed by traditional peacekeeping rules and therefore could use force only in self-defense; and UNITAF, which could use force to protect the delivery of relief supplies. The U.S. government, however, did not wish to see UNITAF remain in Somalia: the objective of the force was to deliver the relief supplies, feed the starving people of Somalia, and then withdraw.

UNOSOM II

Once UNITAF had achieved a level of stability and relief supplies began to reach their targets, the UN assumed responsibility for security in Somalia in May 1993 with the creation of a new UN force. It was expected that this force, UNOSOM II, could be made up of as many as 28,000 personnel, although it never reached that number. It was unusual in that Resolution 813 allowed it to use force from the beginning. Its objectives were to maintain peace, disarm warring factions, and protect relief operations. It was expected that UNOSOM II would cover the whole of Somalia and eventually help in rebuilding the country. The United States had expected to leave Somalia once UNITAF had handed over its responsibility to UNOSOM II, but it found that many countries welcomed U.S. support for UNOSOM II. Four thousand U.S. troops remained under UN command to support UNOSOM II's operations. (There was also a separate U.S. unit, a rapid reaction force, but it was not under UN command.)

An Arab member of UNITAF guards Somalis near a food distribution center in Mogadishu, 1993.

U.S. forces on patrol in
Somalia in 1993

Media Watch

UN moves to crack down on Somali warlords
The search for fugitive General Mohammed Farah Aidid

With Mogadishu smoldering in anger and violence, the United Nations peacekeeping operation in Somalia is finding that its fundamental mission to restore order is proving increasingly elusive.

But it is premature to say that the United Nations effort has bogged down in the quagmire of a protracted guerrilla war.

Many United Nations and United States officials say they believe that the United Nations can turn the situation around and restore peace to Mogadishu if it quickly arrests the fugitive Somali clan leader, Gen. Mohammed Farah Aidid. Time, however, is widely thought to be running out.

General Aidid, accused by the United Nations of masterminding the ambush that killed 24 Pakistani peacekeepers on June 5, has been in hiding for more than three weeks. The United Nations has hit his headquarters and other command centers with massive air and ground attacks. It is offering a $25,000 reward for information leading to his capture.

Yet Aidid has continued to organize guerrilla strikes against the United Nations and has severely weakened the organization's credibility in Somalia…

Gen. Aidid's gunmen have also been blamed for attacks that killed 11 other United Nations soldiers and wounded 137 in the last five weeks, plunging Mogadishu back into the chaos that prevailed before an American-led military force intervened in December.

Source: *New York Times,* July 13 and 15, 1993

The problems of UNOSOM II and the remaining U.S. troops were highlighted in June 1993 when 24 troops from UNOSOM II were killed in an ambush by Somalis, probably those under the leadership of General Mohammed Farah Aidid, the strongest warlord in Somalia. General Aidid and his supporters had denounced the UN intervention as interference in the

Members of UNOSOM II on duty in Somalia in 1993

internal affairs of the country and warned the UN to confine itself to relief work. This attitude underlined the difficulties the UN was facing in Somalia. The peace in the country could not be guaranteed unless the warring groups could be disarmed and the leaders rounded up. The UN tried to do this throughout 1993 but were unsuccessful. The UN and the U.S. troops, under separate command, resorted to heavy attacks, including the use of helicopter gunships, against the warring groups. Many of these attacks were ineffective since the UN force and the U.S. troops who had remained in Somalia were unable to pinpoint the position of these groups accurately. They often attacked the wrong targets and killed innocent civilians. In September, two hundred people, mostly women and children, were killed when a U.S. combat helicopter fired on a crowd. These incidents created a very bad image for the UN and led to tension within UNOSOM II because some of the contributing countries, particularly Italy, criticized the way in which operations were being carried out. The situation reached a crisis in October 1993 when, in an attempt to capture supporters of General Aidid, 18 U.S. troops were killed and more than 70 injured. President Bill Clinton stated that the United States intended to withdraw all its troops from Somalia. This prompted other states to announce their intention to abandon UNOSOM II.

Problems highlighted by UN action in Somalia
The experience of UNOSOM II showed that any decision to use force by the UN needs careful consideration.

Because UNOSOM II was given the right to use force from the start in order to achieve its objectives, it was not always clear when it was acting as a peacekeeping force and when it was acting as a coercive force. It therefore lost the support of many of the Somalis whom it was trying to help.

Many of the troops in UNOSOM II were neither well-trained nor experienced. There was a breakdown in communications in the country between many of the units, and there were problems over command and control of the force. The UN was shown to lack the information that it needed in order to identify the many warring groups and their locations. Consequently, small but well-armed groups were able to inflict damage on a UN force that was not trained for confrontation.

Because of problems such as these, UN casualties in enforcement operations are always likely to be greater than those in peacekeeping operations. Governments must expect this to be the case if they provide troops for future UN operations that move from peacekeeping to enforcement in the course of the operation.

Somali women express their views on UN action in Somalia. Note that the signs are written in English rather than Somali, which is Somalia's official language.

CONCLUSION

The UN's record as a peacekeeper since 1945 has been a mixed one, and the UN has faced many problems in trying to keep the peace.

First of all, in any situation, there needs to be an agreement to keep the peace. If the actions of the UN are not supported by those involved in the dispute, there is very little that a UN peacekeeping force can do.

One of the most important reasons why some of the UN peacekeeping operations have failed has been the attitudes of major powers in the Security Council. During the Cold War, the superpowers were reluctant to allow the UN to operate in areas under their influence. Since the end of the Cold War, the UN has intervened in wars in many parts of the globe, but often without the political, financial, and military support necessary to achieve its peacekeeping goals.

Political support from member states is essential if a UN force is to be set up and to operate successfully. In addition, a UN force needs a clear mandate and instructions on what it is expected to do and achieve.

The UN General Assembly Building in New York City. It is located between First Avenue and Roosevelt Drive and between East 42nd Street and East 48th Street. The General Assembly, Secretariat, Conference, and Library buildings are all interconnected. Tours are available of the buildings for the general public.

Once in the field of operations, it must also have the long-term support of the major powers to back it up if it is prevented from carrying out its tasks.

Throughout the 1990s, although the international community has felt that something had to be done in response to wars across the world, it has not always been prepared to give full support to UN forces in the field of operations.

For many years, the former Soviet Union would not pay for UN peacekeeping and, in the 1980s, the United States began to fall behind in its contributions to the UN budget. Although the end of the Cold War changed the attitude of the superpowers toward paying for the UN, there is still a large gap in the UN peacekeeping budget.

Dr. Boutros Boutros-Ghali, the sixth UN Secretary General, on a visit to Africa

Fact File

How peacekeeping is funded
The UN is financed by assessed (or imposed) contributions and by voluntary contributions from member states. Assessed contributions cover the UN budget and the special peacekeeping accounts set up to support each peacekeeping force. The amount each nation contributes to the regular UN budget is linked to its national income, while the amount it pays to the peacekeeping accounts are in proportion to the amount it has to pay to the regular budget. Economically powerful countries are assessed by the UN at a higher rate than developing countries and thus pay more.

   The Cyprus force has from the start been financed by voluntary contributions.

This gap has become larger as the number of UN peacekeeping forces has increased. By the middle of 1994, there were more than 70,000 troops and civilian police from 70 countries serving with UN peacekeeping forces across the world. The cost of these operations was $3.2 billion per year, yet over one third of these annual costs had not been paid by member states. By October 1994, the United States owed $453 million and Russia owed $569 million.

The U.S. government was reluctant to see the UN incur further debts through the creation of more peacekeeping forces, and countries are now reluctant to provide military and civilian police forces for peacekeeping operations because they fear they will not be paid by the UN for their contributions.

Governments are also concerned that their troops will be placed in great danger in some of these operations. This has been particularly true of the UN forces in Bosnia and Somalia, where the UN has operated in the middle of civil wars.

Members of the Irish contingent to UNFICYP (right) at a signal post in Famagusta, Cyprus, 1964

Fact File

The United Nations Force in Cyprus (UNFICYP)

UNFICYP is an interesting example of a UN peacekeeping force that began as an internal force but, following a change in circumstances, successfully changed into a border patrol force.

In 1960, the island of Cyprus gained independence from Great Britain. The island was mostly Greek, but it had a large Turkish minority (18 percent of the population). By 1964, the government of the island had broken down as a result of Greek-Cypriot and Turkish-Cypriot rivalries. Fighting broke out between the two communities and there was a danger that Greece and Turkey would go to war over the island. In order to prevent this, in March 1964 the UN sent a force of peacekeepers to Cyprus to monitor a cease-fire, to assist in the restoration of law and order, and to keep the peace.

Although there were periodic outbursts of fighting, the UN force performed well until 1974. In that year, the Turks, provoked by a Greek movement to unite the island with the rest of Greece, invaded Cyprus. Since then, the island has been divided into two parts and UNFICYP has patrolled the border between the Turkish Republic of Northern Cyprus and the remainder of the island.

66 99

• • •

The Future
"To remain calm in the face of provocation, to maintain composure when under attack, the United Nations troops, officers and soldiers alike, must show a special kind of courage, one that is more difficult to come by than the ordinary kind. Our United Nations troops have been put to the test and have emerged triumphant."

Source: Javier Perez de Cuellar, UN Secretary General 1982–91

Following the end of the Cold War, many people became optimistic about what the UN might be able to do in the future. Some of this optimism was lost when the UN failed in its aims in Bosnia and Somalia. Yet the UN can only be as efficient and as strong as its member states wish it to be.

There are some improvements that could be made in the organization of the UN that would assist it in its peacekeeping role. This includes providing better military intelligence for the Secretary General. Member states could also identify and select troops within their own armed forces to be available for UN duty should the UN require them. Until the international community reaches an agreement about what the role of the UN should be and is prepared to support that role, UN peacekeeping will remain a valuable but limited service to world peace.

The value of the UN's work is recognized. UN Secretary General Perez de Cuellar receives the Nobel Peace Prize in Oslo, Norway, in 1988 on behalf of UN peacekeeping forces.

NOBEL PEACE PRIZE 1988

UNITED NATIONS PEACE-KEEPING

GLOSSARY

Axis Powers The coalition of Germany, Italy, and Japan, which fought the Allies (Great Britain and the Commonwealth and, from 1941, the United States, Russia, and China) in World War II.

Balkans The area of southeastern Europe consisting of the former Yugoslavia, Bulgaria, Greece, Albania, part of Romania, and European Turkey.

bloc A group of states or countries that have the same political or military interests.

coalition A group of states that ally with one another to achieve a particular goal.

Cold War The bad relations between the United States and the Soviet Union and their respective allies from 1946–89.

Czechoslovakian Revolution A revolution that occurred in 1968 when the Communist Party in Czechoslovakia tried to reform the political system. The Soviet Union saw this as a threat to Communism, so troops from the Warsaw Pact countries were sent to overthrow the new government.

ethnic conflict Fighting among groups because of national, religious, or cultural differences.

ethnic cleansing The forced removal of a particular group of people from an area because of their national, religious, or cultural identity.

Hungarian Uprising A popular uprising against Communism in Hungary in 1956, which was brutally put down by the Soviet army.

The League of Nations An international organization that aimed to achieve world peace. It was set up in 1919, after World War I. The United States was not a member. The League was replaced by the UN.

mandate The set of tasks that the UN gives to a peacekeeping or observer force and the rules within which it must work.

Nationalist China China from 1928–49 when it was ruled by a Nationalist government. This government was overthrown by the Communists, led by Mao Tse-tong, in 1949. The Nationalists retreated to the island of Taiwan and set up a government there.

North Atlantic Treaty Organization (NATO) An alliance of 16 countries, including the United States, created in 1949 to defend Europe against any military threat from the Soviet bloc.

observer forces UN forces who have a limited role, normally the monitoring and reporting of incidents. These forces are generally small and carry limited arms. Peacekeeping forces are larger, have wider responsibilities, and are better armed, but can still use force only in self-defense.

People's Republic of China The government that was set up in 1949 by the Chinese Communist Party (see *Nationalist China*).

preventive deployment The policy put forward by UN Secretary General Boutros Boutros-Ghali that allowed the UN to be involved in disputes at an early stage before they become too big to resolve easily.

resolution A statement of intentions put forward by the UN General Assembly and the Security Council, which is then voted on by member states.

trusteeship The authority given to a state to look after the well-being of another state or territory.

ultimatum A final demand from one or more states to another state or states that, if not agreed to, will lead to some further action, such as war.

UN High Commission for Refugees (UNHCR) An office of the UN General Assembly that seeks to monitor and assist people who have fled from their homeland.

UN Secretary General The chief administrator of the UN who often has to act as a political leader but is neither a head of government nor a head of state.

Vietnam War A war fought by the United States and the Republic of South Vietnam from 1964–75 against North Vietnam and the Vietcong Communist organization.

Warsaw Pact An alliance of seven Communist states in Europe—the Soviet Union, East Germany, Poland, Czechoslovakia, Hungary, Romania, Bulgaria—that existed during the Cold War period.

World War II A world war fought from 1939–45 between the Allies and the Axis powers (see *Axis Powers*).

FURTHER READING

King, John. *Conflict in the Middle East.* Conflicts. New York: New Discovery Books, 1993.

Pollard, Michael. *The United Nations.* Organizations That Help the World. New York: New Discovery Books, 1995.

Ricciuti, Edward. *Somalia: A Crisis of Famine and War.* Headliners. Brookfield, CT: Millbrook Press, 1993.

A list of publications by the UN is available from United Nations Publications, 2 United Nations Plaza, Room 853, New York, NY 10017.

UNITED NATIONS PEACEKEEPING AND OBSERVER FORCES SINCE 1945

in chronological order

Forces created during the Cold War
UNTSO United Nations Truce Supervision Organization
UNMOGIP United Nations Military Observer Group in India and Pakistan
UNEF I United Nations Emergency Force I
UNOGIL United Nations Observer Group in Lebanon
ONUC United Nations Operation in the Congo.
UNSF United Nations Security Force
UNYOM United Nations Yemen Observer Mission
UNFICYP United Nations Force in Cyprus
UNIPOM United Nations India–Pakistan Observer Mission
UNEF II United Nations Emergency Force II
UNDOF United Nations Disengagement Observer Force
UNIFIL United Nations Interim Force in Lebanon

Forces created since the end of the Cold War
UNGOMAP United Nations Good Offices Mission to Afghanistan and Pakistan
UNIIMOG United Nations Iran–Iraq Military Observer Group
UNAVEM I United Nations Angola Verification Mission I
UNTAG United Nations Transition Assistance Group
ONUCA United Nations Observer Group in Central America
UNAVEM II United Nations Angola Verification Mission II
UNIKOM United Nations Iraq–Kuwait Observer Mission
MINURSO United Nations Mission for the Referendum in Western Sahara
ONUSA United Nations Observer Mission in El Salvador
UNAMIC United Nations Advanced Mission in Cambodia
UNTAC United Nations Transitional Authority in Cambodia
UNPROFOR United Nations Protection Force in Yugoslavia
ONUMOZ United Nations Mission in Mozambique
UNOSOM I United Nations Operation in Somalia
UNOSOM II United Nations Operation in Somalia II
UNOMUR United Nations Observer Mission in Uganda–Rwanda
UNAMIR United Nations Mission in Rwanda
UNOMIL United Nations Observer Mission in Liberia
UNOMIG United Nations Observer Mission in Georgia
UNMIH United Nations Mission in Haiti
UNOMSA United Nations Observer Mission in South Africa

INDEX

Numbers in **bold** indicate subjects shown
in pictures as well as in the text.